PINGU

and His Family

BBC BOOKS

Pingu was up early. For the first time, ever, he was going to help his dad deliver the post.

not a little brother, but a little sister!
"We'll call her Pinga," said Pingu's mum.

"You can watch your little brother coming out of the egg, now," she told him.
The midwife gently tapped the shell of the egg and out came...

“Stop that, Pingu,” scolded his mum. “It won't be long before you have a little brother to play with.”

The midwife listened to the heartbeat inside the egg with her stethoscope. In her hurry, she had lost her cap. "Can I try it on?" asked Pingu.

Pingu climbed on to the roof of the igloo to watch for the midwife. As she came skating towards him, Pingu opened the door and called out, "Be quick! My little brother is ready to hatch!"

"I'll phone the midwife straight away so that she can help him come out completely," said Pingu's dad.

"Be quick!" cried his mum. "The cracks in the shell are getting bigger!"

"Ouch! That hurt!" cried Pingu's dad, jumping up. "Come and see, Pingu. The little rascal has already put his beak through the shell!"

Pingu's mum was feeling very nervous. The telephone was ringing, the kettle was whistling. "It's chaotic in this house," thought Pingu. "There's never a moment's peace."

THE NEW ARRIVAL

"Hey, come and look!" called Pingu's mum, excitedly. "The egg is about to break!"
"Not yet, be patient," replied his dad and he sat down on the egg to finish off the incubation.

Pingu's mum called him in to try on his new red hat. "Really, Pingu," she said. "You may be naughty sometimes, but you really are the most handsome little penguin!"

But his mum did not scold him. "No harm has been done luckily, but now you must tidy up the room, Pingu!"

Luckily Pingu's dad caught the egg in a net and put it gently back in its place. Pingu hid in a cupboard as he was sure his parents would be very cross with him.

Pingu bounced just a little too hard and the egg went flying towards the door, just as his mum and dad rushed in!
"My egg!" cried his mum in horror.

Meanwhile, the house was in turmoil with Pingu and the egg see-sawing happily in the middle of the room.

Pingu's mum and dad heard strange noises coming from the igloo. They ran back inside to find out what was going on.

Pingu tried to catch the egg but it was too fast for him. "Come back here, you're making me cross!" he shouted. But the egg wouldn't listen.

When the music stopped, Pingu sat down to rest ... but, suddenly, someone tapped him from behind.
Terrified, Pingu swung round. "Who is it?" he asked.

But, Pingu's favourite music was not the kind of music to listen to sitting down, and soon he was up and dancing all around the room. He didn't notice that the egg was doing the same thing!

Pingu soon grew bored. "Really," he thought, "I could easily sit on the egg *and* listen to music at the same time."

"Pingu, did you hear me?" said his mother crossly, taking off his headset.
"I can't sit on the egg, I'm too small," protested Pingu. "Nonsense," said his mother. "Now sit there and be quiet."

"Pingu," called his mum. "Come and sit on the egg whilst I help to hang out the washing..." But Pingu was listening to his favourite music and didn't hear her.

PINGU LOOKS AFTER THE EGG

A new baby was expected in Pingu's family. While she sat incubating a large egg, Pingu's mum was knitting a new hat for Pingu.

Pingu was very happy to be home after such a busy and exciting morning.
"Pingu is a very good boy, we should be proud of him!" said his dad. "He helped me a lot this morning."

Pingu skipped nearly all the way home. He ducked low as he passed Mrs Roller's house, as he saw her beating a carpet that had a picture of a small penguin on it.

"I carried lots and lots of big parcels, all by myself!" Pingu proudly told the Post Office manager. "I'm going to be a postman, too, when I grow up. And, I'll drive the truck!"

By midday, all the post had been delivered. "Hold on tight, little Pingu," called his dad, driving very fast back along the bumpy snow track.

Mrs McGreedy hardly managed to finish opening her parcel before her three little penguins snatched out their favourite cakes.

At the next igloo Pingu was knocked flying by the absent-minded Professor Threehorn.

"Luckily, not many letters are as sad as that one!" said Pingu's dad, as they continued on their round.

But at the next igloo, they delivered a sad letter to a frail, old penguin, whose cousin had died.

At the first igloo Pingu delivered a birthday present. The little penguin was delighted.

"This is going to be hard work," panted Pingu, as he loaded the last big parcel on to the truck.

"I'm the postman's helper," Pingu told the Post Office manager. "I'm in charge of the parcels." "Excellent. There's lots of post to deliver today."

"Good morning, Mrs Roller," said Pingu's dad as they passed their new neighbour's house.